Reward Stickers

Note to Parents

1) Most of the activities in this book should be at an appropriate developmental level, which will allow your child to do them independently. But don't hesitate to help them! When parents are involved in the learning process, it increases a child's intellectual curiosity and creates a more effective, supportive learning environment.

2) To support your child's learning, review the **"To Parents"** section featured below the instructions. These tips offer parents effective ways to explain the activity to your child.

3) As mentioned on the previous page, this book is divided into three steps. The first step, coloring freely, shifts to the second step, coloring in a specified place, but even then it does not matter if your child's coloring goes out of the frame. Prioritize the freedom to enjoy coloring rather than being exact about it. The repetition of these activities will lead to the next step. Another feature of this book is that the front and back sides are the same scene. The back side is slightly more difficult, offering more space to color than the front side. If the back side is difficult, your child can come back to do it later.

4) When your child finishes each activities, let them choose a **reward sticker** to put on the page. Be sure to also praise your child's good work! Be specific with your praise, saying something like, "You did a good job!" or "You were very patient!"

Hold a Crayon

Drawing Lines or Letters

Grip the crayon between your thumb and index finger, and then support it with your middle finger.

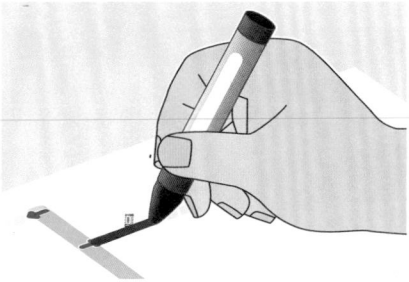

Coloring

Grip the top of the crayon firmly between your thumb and index finger.

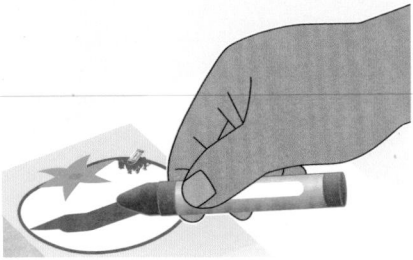

How to Hold a Pencil

Hold the pencil at a 60-degree angle.

Hold the pencil just above the sharpened part. Be careful not to put too much pressure on your fingers.

Grip the pencil between your thumb and index finger, and then support it with your middle finger.

For writing practice, use a shorter, fatter pencil, as it is easier to grip.

Caution: The paper in this book can be sharp. Take care when handling. This book contains small stickers. Keep out of mouths.

Watermelon Seeds

Level 1 ★☆☆

Example

Black

Draw dots on the watermelon to add seeds.

To Parents Allow your child to hold the crayon however they want. You can show them how to make dots before they begin.

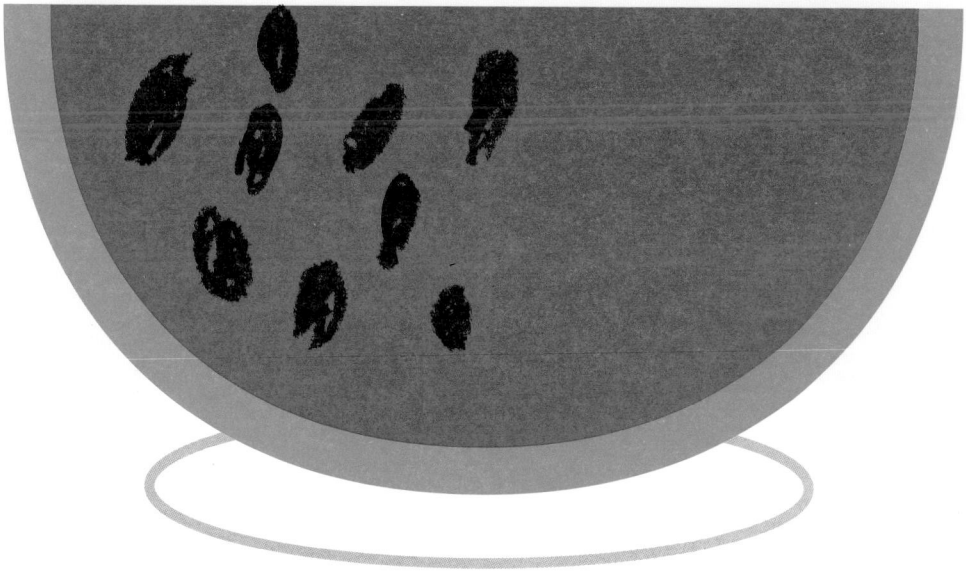

Watermelon Seeds

Good job!

Draw more seeds.

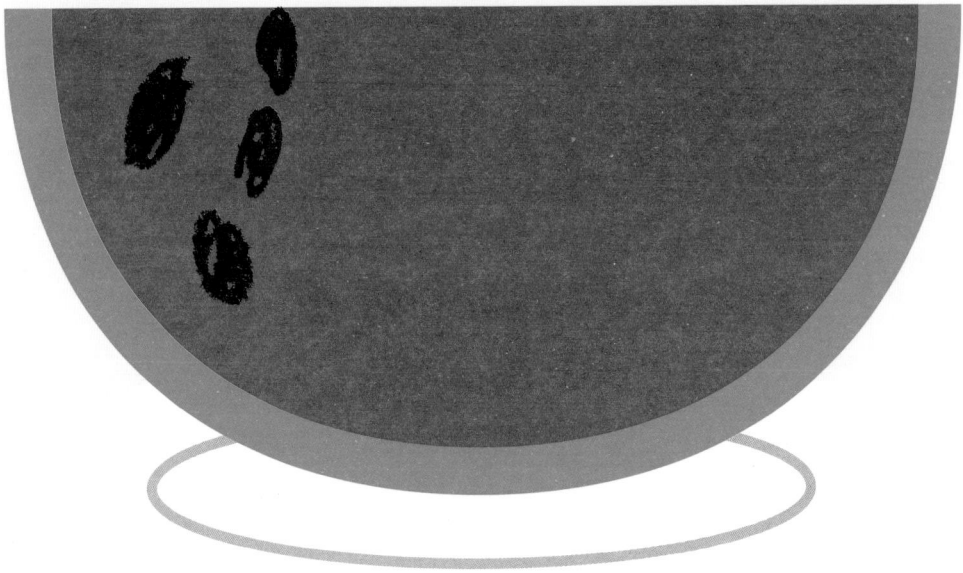

Strawberry Seeds

Level 1 ★☆☆

Example

Black

Draw dots on the strawberries to add seeds.

To Parents Because children of this age usually do not apply much pressure when writing, have them use crayons that are easy to color with.

Strawberry Seeds

Draw more seeds.

Playing in the Sand

Level 1 ★☆☆

Example

Brown

Draw dots to add sand to the pile.

Playing in the Sand

Good job!

Draw more sand.

Dad's Beard

Example

Black

Draw dots to finish Dad's beard.

To Parents Learning to draw dots is similar to learning to draw short vertical lines. It's okay if some dots are a little longer than others.

Dad's Beard

Good job!

Draw more of Dad's beard.

Frozen Treat

Draw syrup on the ice.

Example

Red

To Parents Let your child draw however they want. It's okay if they mix horizontal lines, vertical lines, and diagonal lines. Using a crayon helps them develop fine motor skills and enriches their creativity.

Frozen Treat

Good job!

Draw more syrup.

Fluffy Clouds

Draw clouds in the sky.

Example

White

To Parents Your child may want to use a black or gray crayon to draw the clouds. It's wonderful if they know clouds are also these colors.

Fluffy Clouds

Good job!

Draw more clouds.

Red Tulip

Color the empty space on the flower.

Example

Red

To Parents It is okay if your child colors outside of the white shape. It is more important that they select the right color.

Red Tulip

Good job!

Color one more flower.

Green Leaf

Color the empty space on the leaf.

Example

Green

To Parents Ask your child which color they should use to fill in the leaf.

Green Leaf

Good job!

Color one more leaf.

Sweet Apple

Color the empty space on the apple.

To Parents Tell your child to hold the paper lightly with their free hand while coloring.

Sweet Apple

Good job!

Color one more apple.

Delicious Bananas

Color the empty spaces on the bananas.

Level 2 ★★☆

Delicious Bananas

Good job!

Color more bananas.

Crisp Cucumbers

Color the empty spaces on the cucumbers.

Level 2 ★★☆

Example

Green

Crisp Cucumbers

Good job!

Color more cucumbers.

Flying Butterfly

Color the empty spaces on the butterfly's wings.

Level 2 ★★☆

Yellow

Flying Butterfly

Color more wings.

Good job!

Fresh Tomatoes

Color the empty spaces on the tomatoes.

Level 2 ★★☆

Example

Red

Fresh Tomatoes

Good job!

Color two more tomatoes.

Level 2 ★★☆

Chirping Chicks

Color the empty spaces on the chicks.

Chirping Chicks

Good job!

Color two more chicks.

Watering Flowers

Level 1 ★☆☆

Example

Light blue

Draw lines to add more water.

To Parents This activity focuses on drawing straight lines. Show your child how to draw a line while saying, "Let's water the flowers!"

Watering Flowers

Good job!

Draw more water.

Falling Rain

Draw lines of rain.

Light blue

To Parents Encourage your child to hold the tip of their crayon, just like they would hold a pencil. This allows them to draw lines more easily. But remember not to force them.

Falling Rain

Draw more rain.

Good job!

Puppy Race

Draw lines from ● to ●.

Favorite color

To Parents This activity challenges your child to draw a line from start to end in a designated area.

Puppy Race

Draw lines again.

Fishing Fun

Draw fishing lines from ● to ●.

Favorite color

Fishing Fun

Good job!

Draw lines again.

Playful Sea Lions

Level 2 ★★☆

Example

Green

Color the empty space of the ball.

To Parents Encourage your child to color along the outline of the ball first. This will help them color within the ball.

Playful Sea Lions

Good job!

Color two more balls.

Crunchy Carrots

Color the carrot.

Level 2 ★★☆

Example

Orange

Crunchy Carrots

Good job!

Color two more carrots.

Cozy Socks

Color the sock.

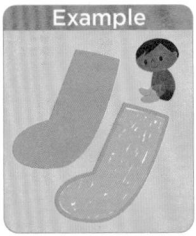

Light green

Cozy Socks

Good job!

Color two more socks.

Orange Tree

Color the orange.

Orange Tree

Good job!

Color three more oranges.

Round Grapes

Color the grapes.

Example

Purple

Round Grapes

Good job!

Color more grapes.

Bear Buddies

Color the bear's face.

Example

Brown

To Parents When your child colors larger areas, encourage them to slant the crayon. This allows them to easily color more space.

Bear Buddies

Good job!

Color one more bear.

Striped Shirt

Example

Yellow

Draw horizontal lines on the shirt.

To Parents This activity practices drawing long horizontal lines. Encourage your child to draw each line to the end, even if it's shaky or uneven.

Striped Shirt

Draw more horizontal lines.

Good job!

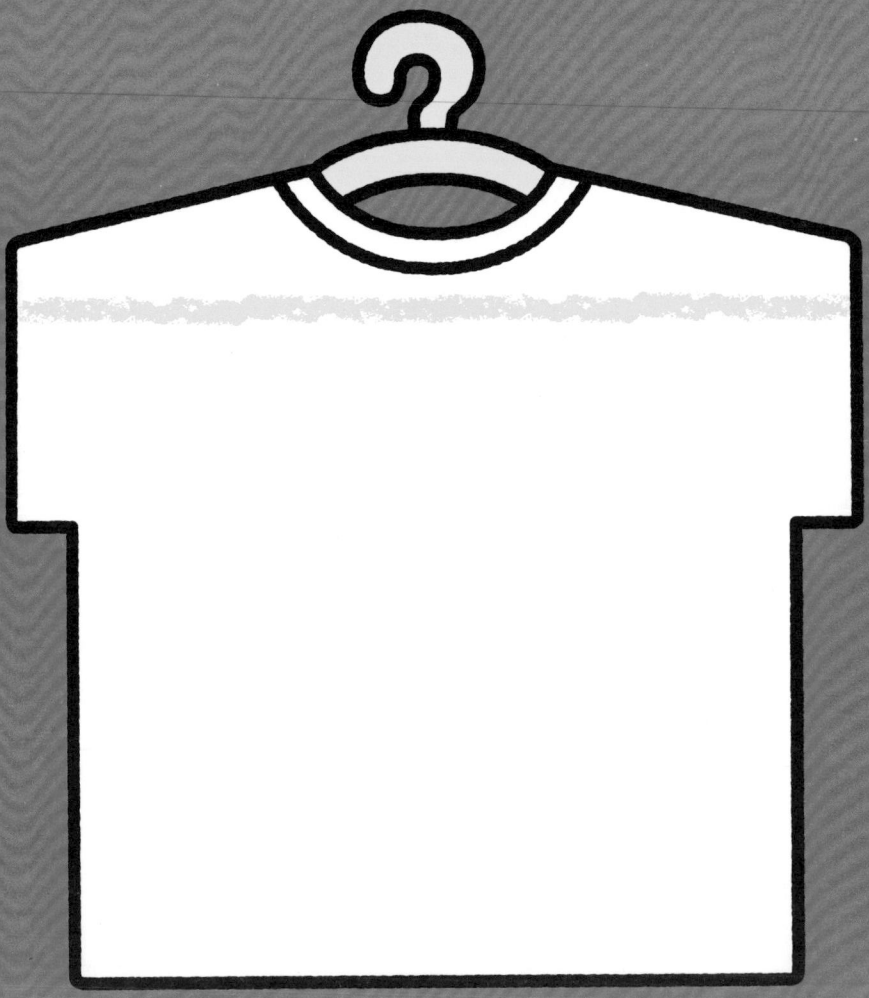

Level 2 ★★☆

Fancy Dress

Draw diagonal lines on the dress.

Example

Pink

To Parents If it's difficult for your child to draw a diagonal line, place your hand on their hand to guide them.

Fancy Dress

Good job!

Draw more diagonal lines.

Level 2 ★★☆

Striped Truck

Example

Green

Draw horizontal lines on the truck.

To Parents This activity allows your child to draw straight horizontal lines in larger areas. Encourage them to draw the lines closer together, so the space between them is narrow.

Striped Truck

Good job!

Draw more horizontal lines.

Sweet Melons

Draw vertical and horizontal lines on the melon.

Green

Sweet Melons

Good job!

Draw more lines.

Walking Crabs

Example

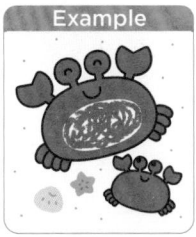

Red

What color is a crab? Color it.

To Parents It is okay if your child colors outside of the white space.

Walking Crabs

Good job!

Color two more crabs.

Night Sky

What color are the moon and the star?
Color them.

Example

Yellow

Night Sky

Color one more moon and star.

Good job!

Speedy Fire Truck

What color is a fire truck? Color it.

Level 2 ★★☆

Example

Red

Speedy Fire Truck

Good job!

Color one more fire truck.

Lemon and Orange

What colors are the pieces of fruit?
Color them.

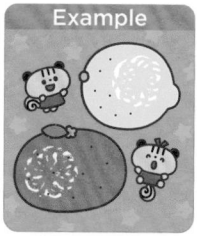

To Parents In this activity, your child will use two different colors. Before coloring, ask your child to name the colors of the lemon and the orange.

Lemon and Orange

Good job!

Color more fruit.

Lettuce and Green Pepper

Level 3 ★★★

What colors are the vegetables?
Color them.

Lettuce and Green Pepper

Good job!

Color more vegetables.

Bright Flowers

Color one flower's petals pink and the other flower's center yellow.

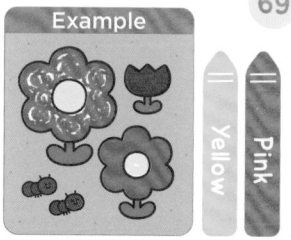

To Parents Ask your child what color they need to paint each part, referring to the example. When they are done coloring, praise your child by saying, "You made beautiful flowers."

Bright Flowers

Good job!

Color more flowers.

Summer Sunflower

Color the petals yellow and the leaf green.

Summer Sunflower

Good job!

Color one more sunflower.

Dinner Time

Draw dots to put food in the cat's dish.

Example

Brown

To Parents It's important to show your child how to hold a crayon properly, but do not force it. Your child will get the hang of it as their fine motor skills develop.

Snack Time

Good job!

Draw more cat food.

Dress-up Fun

Example

Light blue

Draw dots on the doll's outfit.

To Parents This activity lets your child practice drawing dots at equal intervals. Refer to the girls in the example to draw.

Dress-up Fun

Good job!

Draw more dots.

Rocket Launch

Draw lines to add smoke.

Example

Blue

To Parents It's okay to draw the lines in different directions. Praise your child for drawing a lot of lines rather than for drawing well.

Rocket Launch

Good job!

Draw more smoke.

Under the Sea

Example

Black

Draw an ink cloud to hide the octopus from the shark.

To Parents Before drawing, ask your child what they can draw for the octopus to keep the shark away.

Under the Sea

Good job!

Draw more ink.

Zoom Zoom

Draw lines from ● to ●.

To Parents After tracing the gray line, let your child connect the line to the blue point. It's okay if they can't draw straight.

Zoom Zoom

Good job!

Draw more lines.

Let's Take a Walk!

Draw lines from ● to ●.

Example

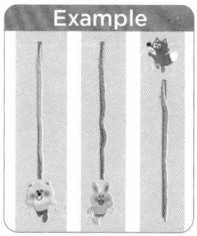

Favorite color

To Parents Encourage your child to practice drawing lines, not only from top to bottom, but also from bottom to top.

Let's Take a Walk!

Good job!

Draw more lines.

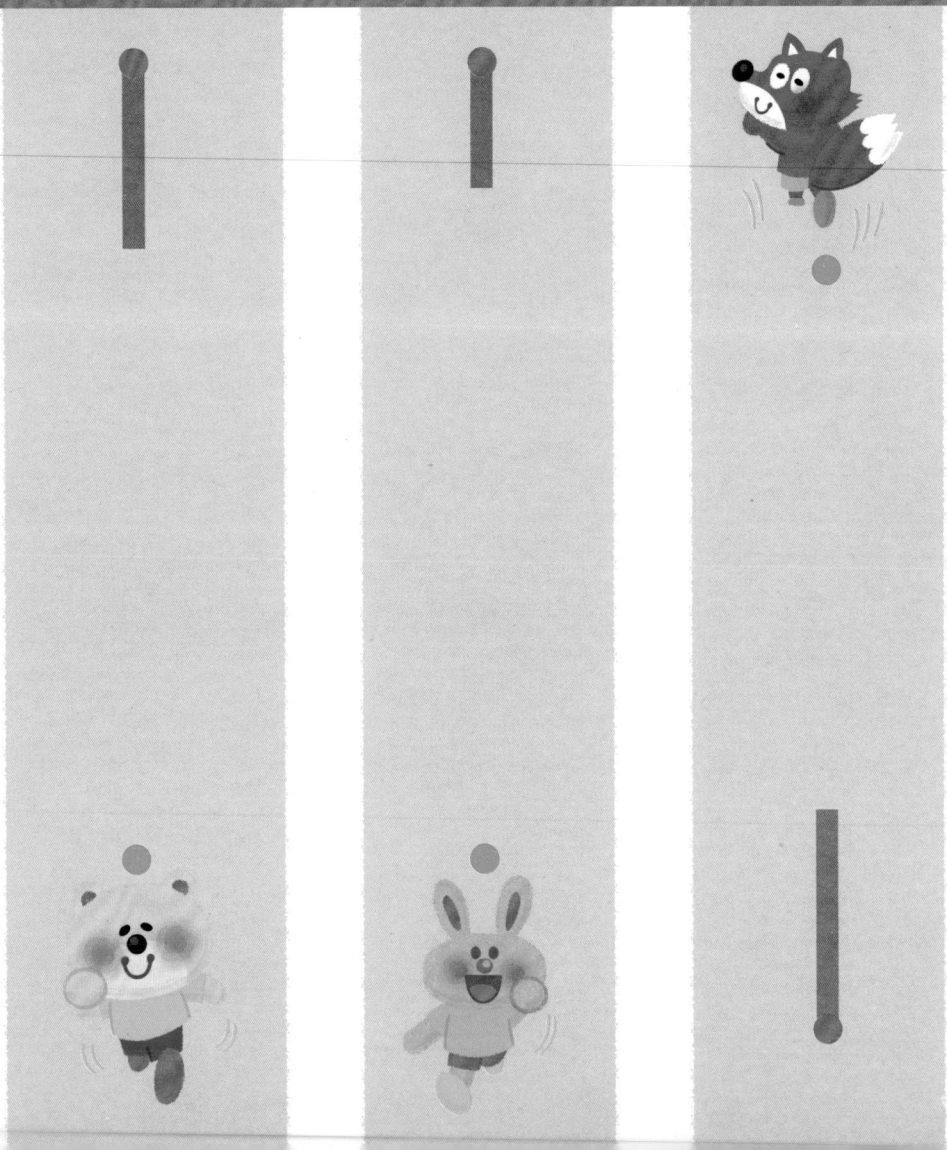

Level 2 ★★☆

Zebra Stripes

Draw lines on the zebras.

Example

Black

Zebra Stripes

Good job!

Draw more lines.

Let's Go Home

Draw a continuous line from ● to ●.

Favorite color

To Parents Tell your child to stop drawing when they need to change direction, then start again.

Let's Go Home

Good job!

Draw another continuous line.

My Way Home

Draw a continuous line from ● to ●.

Favorite color

To Parents It's important that your child learns to begin and end one continuous line. If it's difficult, encourage them to first trace the line with their finger and then draw the line.

My Way Home

Good job!

Draw another continuous line.

Sunny Flowers

Color the center of the flower.

Example

Orange

To Parents Make sure your child practices coloring within the frame.

Sunny Flowers

Good job!

Color one more flower.

Orange Juice

Color the juice.

Orange

Orange Juice

Good job!

Color more juice.

Cow Spots

Color the cow's spots.

Cow Spots

Good job!

Color more spots.

Tiger Pals

Color the tiger.

Level 2 ★★☆

Example

Orange

Tiger Pals

Color one more tiger.

Good job!

Jumping Frogs

Trace each line from ● to ●.

Favorite color

To Parents Because it might be difficult to trace the zigzag line continuously, encourage your child to trace one "mountain" at a time.

Jumping Frogs

Good job!

Trace more zigzag lines.

Hopping Rabbits

Trace each line from ● to ●.

Favorite color

To Parents Because it might be difficult to draw arched lines, allow your child to draw one semicircle at a time. If your child is having a hard time, place your hand on their hand for guidance.

Hopping Rabbits

Good job!

Trace more arched lines.

Puffy Clouds

Trace each line from ● to ●.

Light blue

Puffy Clouds

Good job!

Trace more clouds.

Fluffy Sheep

Trace each line from ● to ●.

Favorite color

To Parents Drawing spiral lines is difficult because the motor function of your child's wrists and fingers are not fully developed. Encourage your child to draw slowly while putting your hand on theirs to help guide them.

Fluffy Sheep

Trace more spiral lines.

A Ball of Yarn

Trace the line from to .

Blue

A Ball of Yarn

Good job!

Trace one more spiral line.

Ice Cream Cones

Trace each line from ● to ●.

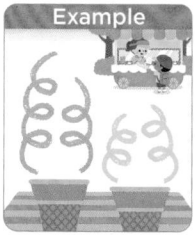

Ice Cream Cones

Good job!

Trace more spiral lines.

Spaghetti

Trace each line from ● to ●.

Orange

To Parents Draw together with your child while saying, "These noodles go around and around." When parents join in the activity, children become more motivated.

Spaghetti

Trace more spiral lines.

Good job!

Big Trees

Color the empty triangles on the trees.

Example

Light green

To Parents Have your child trace the outline of the white triangles, then color them.

Big Trees

Good job!

Color two more trees.

Sunny-Side Up

Example

Yellow

Color the egg yolks.

To Parents Tell your child, "Make two fried eggs, please," and then let them color the yolks.

Sunny-Side Up

Good job!

Color two more egg yolks.

Colorful Balloons

Level 3 ★★★

Example

Favorite color

Color the balloons with your favorite colors.

To Parents Have your child choose their favorite colors. They can also select from the colors of the balloons in the illustration below.

Colorful Balloons

Good job!

Color more balloons.

Sailing the Seas

Color the boat's sails with your favorite colors.

Example

Favorite color

To Parents Have your child trace the outlines of the white triangles, then color them.

Sailing the Seas

Good job!

Color two more sails.

Pretty Hat

Color the hat with your favorite colors.

Example

Favorite color

Pretty Hat

Good job!

Color one more hat.

Warm Mittens

Color the mittens with your favorite color.

Example

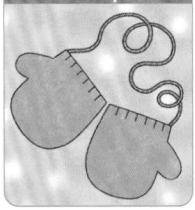

Favorite color

To Parents It's okay to color each mitten with a different color. You can also draw a pattern first and then ask your child to color it.

Warm Mittens

Good job!

Color two more mittens.

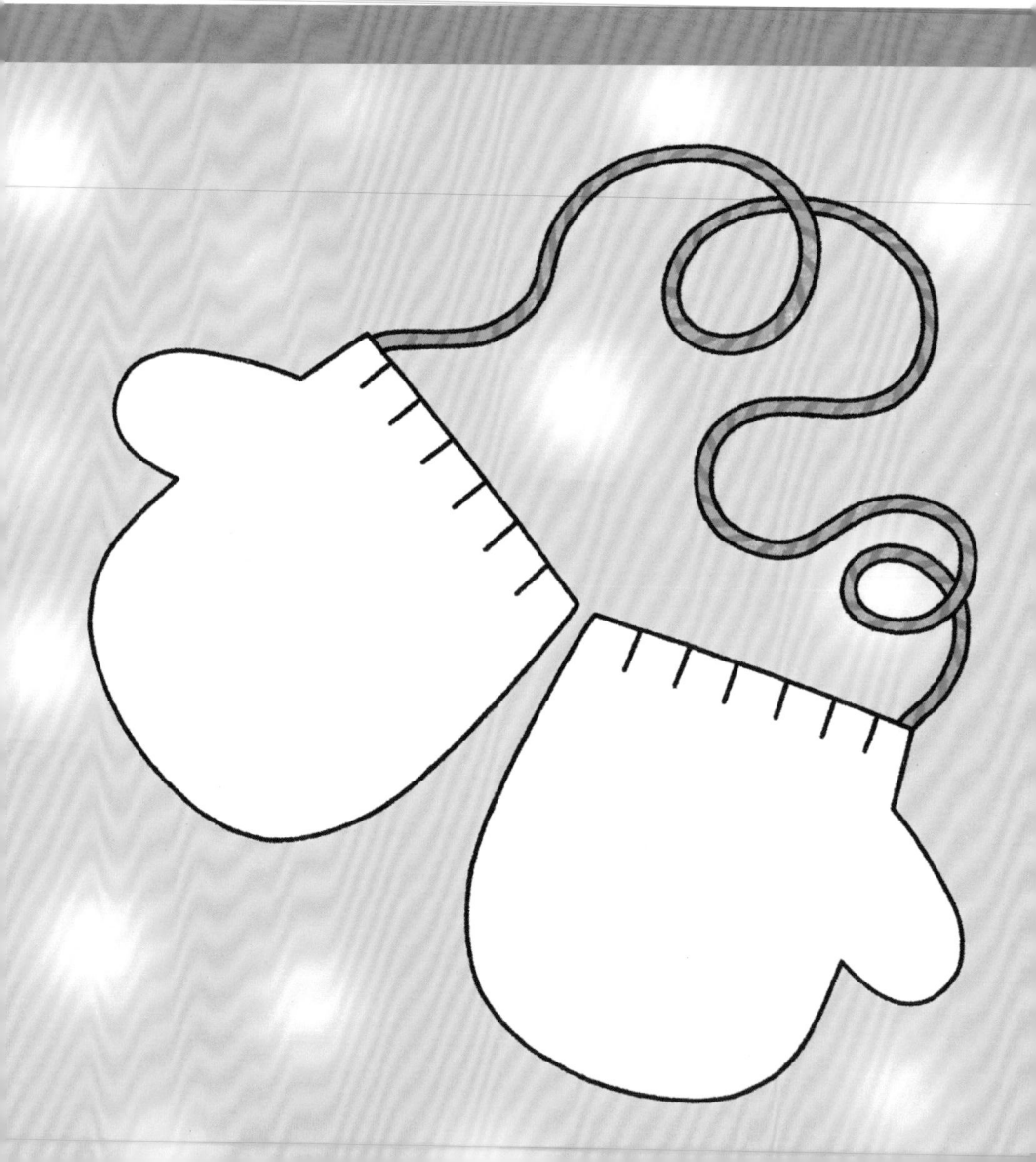

Building Blocks

Color the blocks with your favorite colors.

Example

Favorite color

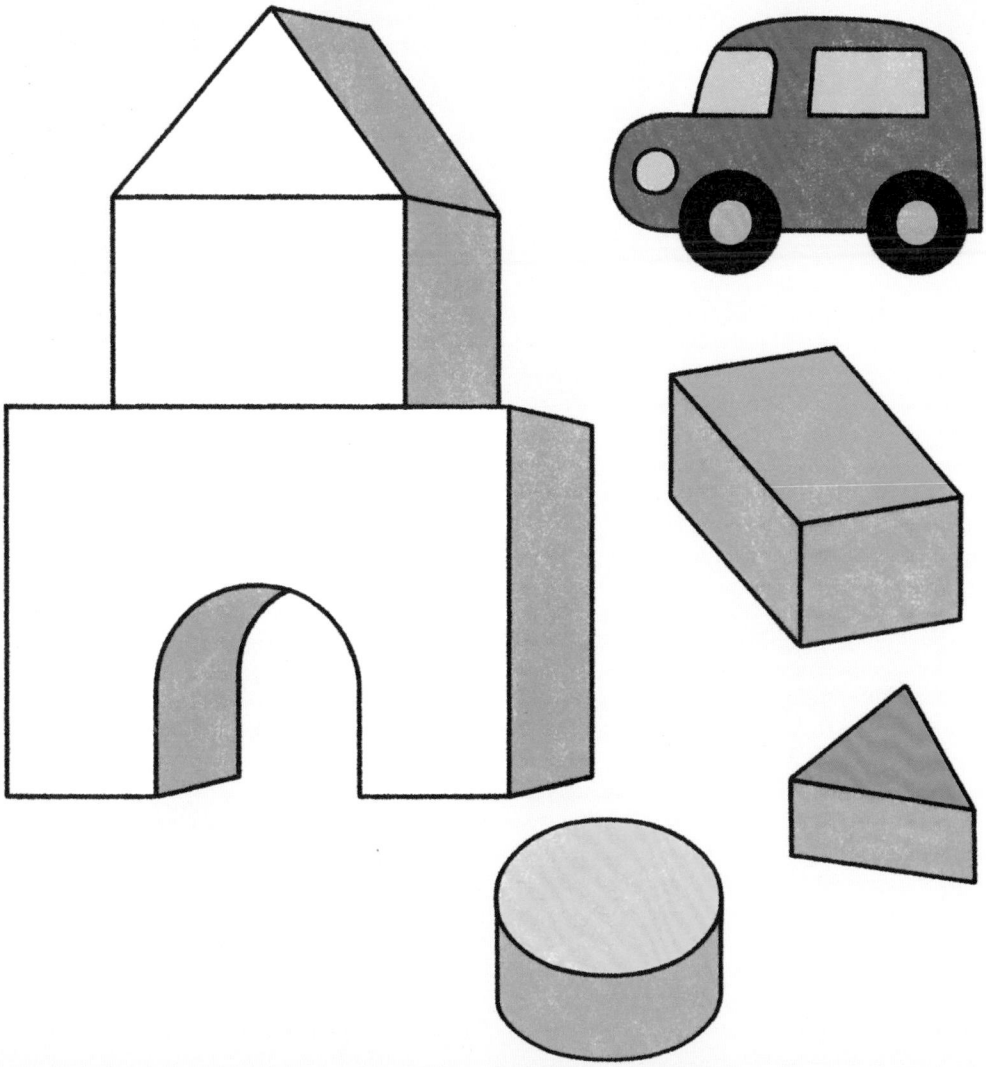

Building Blocks

Good job!

Color more blocks.

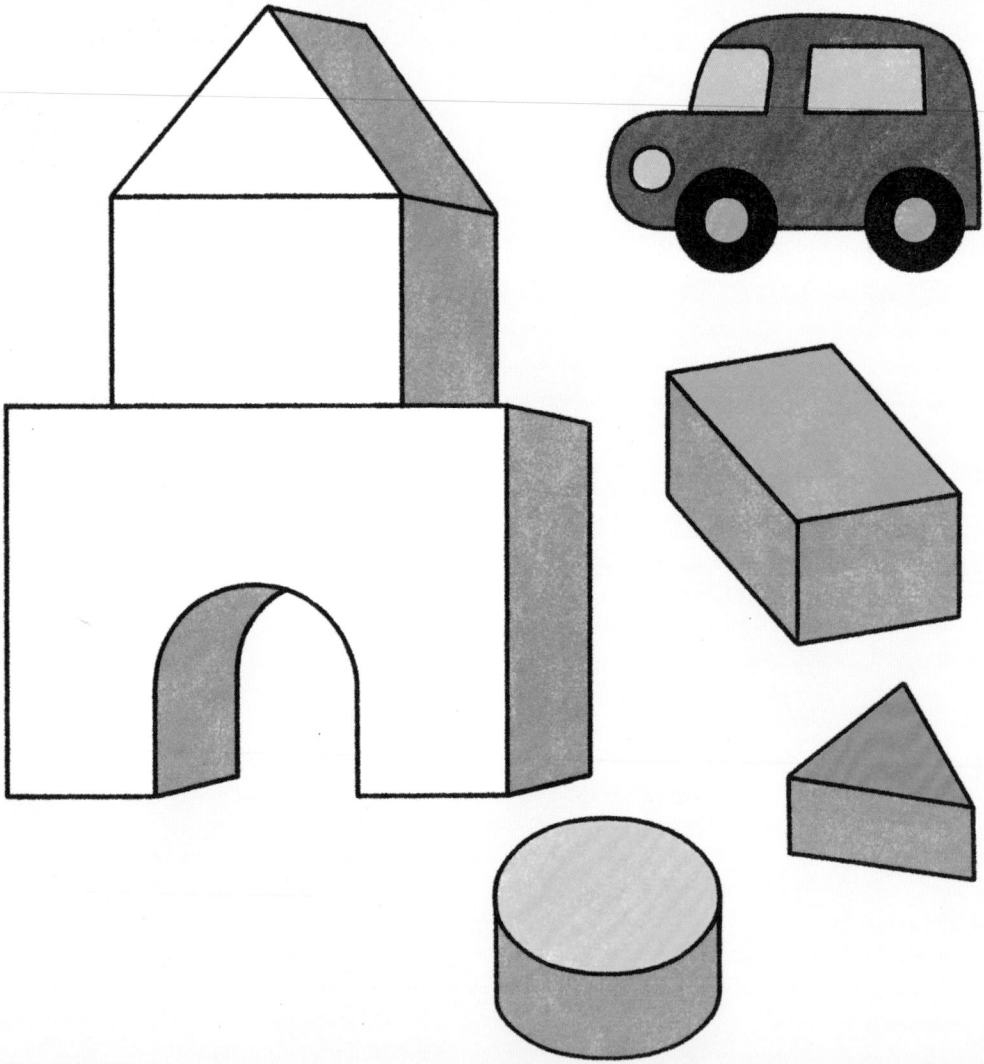

Fish Friends

Color the fish with your favorite colors.

Example

Favorite color

To Parents Your child can also use different colors for the face and fins to make their own original fish.

Fish Friends

Good job!

Color two more fish.